Bipolar Disorder - One Day at a Time

A Devotional Journal for Those

with Bipolar Disorder

by Michele Sexton

<u>Dedication</u>

To my sister, Debi, who always believed in me;

To my husband and best friend, Bill, who stood by my side;

And to my Lord, who wrote the words.

Forward

"And we know that in all things God works for the good of those who love him, who have been called according to his purpose."

--Rom. 8:28 (NIV)

God certainly has worked all things for my good, as I now enjoy a good life, full of happiness and stability. I have a wonderful supporter, a husband who also has bipolar disorder, so he understands me in a way that no one else could.

But it wasn't always that way. There were many times in my life when I felt like adversity was an overwhelming shadow and I felt like I could never come out from underneath it. It was at those times that "God did for me what I could not do for myself," as the saying goes.

By sharing these experiences with you, my hope is that you will see that you are not alone.

In Acts 10:34 (KJV), the Bible tells us that *"God is no respecter of persons."* That means that what He's done for me, He can do for you, too. I have been healed from the pain of my past because of the love of God, and I pray that you will be, too.

"...who have been called according to his purpose." (Rom. 8:28b NIV) God has a purpose for each one of us, in spite of the fact that we have bipolar disorder. My purpose was

to write this book for you, to encourage you through this time in your life.

Through the sharing of my experiences, I pray that you might find hope for yourself. And I hope you'll use the journal sections to record your own thoughts and feelings as you go.

Lord, bless every person who reads this book. May You touch their hearts, heal their pain, and bring joy to their lives. Amen.

Day One

"I have learned, in whatsoever state I am, therewith to be content."

--Phil. 4:11 (KJV)

When Paul wrote those words, it wasn't because he'd had an easy life. Far from it, in fact. Paul was the one with the "thorn in his flesh" that Jesus never removed, remember? (2Cor. 12:7)

We're never told whether it was an actual physical thorn, or whether it was physical or even mental pain, but it did cause him so much pain that he asked Jesus to remove it not once, but three times! Yet Jesus never did. He was only told, *"My grace is sufficient for you, for my power is made perfect in weakness."* (2Cor. 12:9 NIV)

So when I struggle with the question of, "Why doesn't God take away my bipolar disorder?" and I think about all the pain I suffer because of it, I think back to Paul and his thorn.

God had His reasons with Paul, so He must have His reasons with me, too. In spite of the thorn in his side (whether the thorn was literal or figurative), Paul went on to become one of the greatest evangelists of his time.

Ok, so I'm not going to be a great evangelist. But I can still not let my "thorn," my bipolar disorder, stop me from fulfilling God's plan for *my* life.

Paul says, *"I have learned, in whatsoever state I am, therewith to be content."* Paul *learned* – it didn't come overnight, and it didn't come easy. Our hardest lessons always come with pain.

"...whatsoever state..." - his thorn, my bipolar disorder.

"...to be content." Contentment is a state of mind. I don't have to be *happy* that I have bipolar disorder, I just have to *accept* that I do.

Lord, help me to accept bipolar disorder as the "in whatsoever state I am," so, like Paul, "therewith to be content." Amen.

My Thoughts and Feelings

Day Two

*"Come unto me, all ye that labour and are heavy laden, and
I will give you rest."*

--Matt. 11:28 (KJV)

Before I was formally diagnosed with bipolar disorder, I
worked in a hospital as a medical transcriptionist. There
wasn't a lot of physical exertion but, boy, was there a lot of
mental exertion involved in my job!

I never got carpal tunnel syndrome like some of the other
girls, but at the end of an 8-hour shift, my hands, arms, and
back would definitely show signs of physical stress.
Sometimes I would even get migraines from staring at the
computer screen all day. Needless to say, by the time I
would get home from work, I was exhausted!

One day at work, however, I had a "meltdown," and was
taken to the psychiatric institution, where I was diagnosed
with bipolar disorder and put on medication. I was never
able to go back to my job and had to be put on permanent
disability.

All of a sudden, I wasn't a medical transcriptionist any
more – a productive, working member of society. Now I
was a disabled person with a mental illness.

With no more reason to wake up in the morning, I sank into
a deep, dark depression, and I found out what the words
"heavy laden" meant.

I carried fears, worries, and dark, negative thoughts and feelings around with me all day like the heavy concrete of a construction laborer. I'd never known I had those things, because I was too busy working. Oh yes, I found out what it was like to be *"heavy laden."*

I would go to bed every night and cry, because I just wanted to die. I couldn't imagine living like that forever. Then I remembered the Scripture of Matthew 11:28, and gradually the Lord gave me the type of "rest" I so desperately needed.

Lord, thank You that any time my bipolar disorder gets to me and I feel "heavy laden," I can count on You to give me rest. Amen.

My Thoughts and Feelings

Day Three

"Answer me when I call to you, O my righteous God. Give me relief from my distress; be merciful to me and hear my prayer."

--Psa. 4:1 (NIV)

Thank God He didn't answer my prayer to die, because eventually I came out of that deep, dark depression as all of us with bipolar disorder do when we return to what the doctors call our "normal state" (that place between manic and depressed). I learned that there can be *"relief from distress,"* as the Scripture says.

But lest we be fooled, we have to remember that bipolar disorder is a lifetime illness, and does bring with it times of distress. I've learned things that help me manage my disorder – techniques, systems, tips and tricks. I see a psychiatrist and a therapist. And, of course, I take my medication religiously. But without prayer, I'd be as lost as a babe in the woods.

Distress is just a part of bipolar disorder, as it is with any long-term illness, physical or mental. No matter how long we're stable, no matter how high-functioning, no matter how successful our treatment plan, no matter how great our support system, how effective our medications, or how many techniques or systems we've got in place – without prayer, there would never be relief from our distress.

Even long-term stability is not a guarantee that you'll never have another episode – there was a man who was stable for 20 years and then had one. My own mother, who also has bipolar disorder, was stable for 12 years before she had another bipolar episode.

This is because bipolar disorder is not just a mental disorder; it's also a physical one – a chemical imbalance in the brain, and those chemicals can "fire off" at any time and cause a breakthrough episode.

At those times, we truly need God to *"be merciful."* At those times, we truly need to call on God and have Him hear our prayer.

Lord, I am so glad that in times of distress I can call on You and You will give me relief. I'm grateful that You hear my prayers. Amen.

My Thoughts and Feelings

Day Four

"The sacrifices of God are a broken spirit: a broken and a contrite heart, O God, thou wilt not despise."

--Psa. 51:17 (KJV)

I tried to kill myself five times. Well, I didn't so much want to "kill myself" as I just wanted to "be dead." Do you know what I mean? Some attempts were before I was diagnosed with bipolar disorder and some were after. I used different methods, but the intentions were the same – I just wanted relief from my pain.

My life was a study in self-destruction, craziness, depression, alcoholism, drug addiction, abuse, suffering, and pain. Never-ending pain. In my "crazy" mind, I believed that "being dead" was the only way to finally relieve my pain.

Before I was formally diagnosed with bipolar disorder (when I was 44 years old), I always thought I was crazy. I started drinking alcoholically when I was 12 years old, and was an addict by the time I was 14.

It's kind of like the "chicken and the egg" analogy – I'm not sure which came first – was I always an alcoholic and drug addict who happened to get bipolar disorder, or did I always have (undiagnosed) bipolar disorder and used alcohol and drugs to mask the symptoms? Or was I both?

All I knew was, by the time I was 44 years old and received my diagnosis of bipolar disorder, I had a *"broken spirit."* I had a broken life. Well, at least I finally had a name for my "craziness," but that didn't help much. I was still "broken," and believed that no amount of medication could fix that.

That's because the only thing that can fix a *"broken spirit"* is *"a broken and contrite heart,"* according to Psalms 51:17. It was only when I brought both to God and turned them over to Him that I began to heal – that I wanted to live again.

Lord, if it were not for Your great healing powers, my "broken spirit" would have killed me. Thank You for giving me back my life and healing my heart. Amen.

My Thoughts and Feelings

Day Five

"The Lord is close to the brokenhearted and saves those who are crushed in spirit."

--Psa. 34:18 (NIV)

Not long after I was diagnosed with bipolar disorder, I went through a nasty divorce. We had to "split" the children – one week "on," and one week "off."

I lost my home, my car, everything. I was basically homeless with no place to go, no money, and my life all in ruins – all because I was the "crazy" one.

Even though I had been diagnosed, gotten help, been put on medication, and been stabilized, the stigma of having a mental illness still cost me everything.

The life I'd known was taken from me, and I had to start all over again.

I understood completely what the Scripture says about being *"brokenhearted,"* and *"crushed in spirit."*

I had no strong support system – no one to go to for help. I didn't go to an outpatient program. I hadn't joined a bipolar support group. I had long since driven away friends and family. I was lost and alone.

It was certainly a very lonely place in my life.

But the Scripture says that *"The Lord is close to the brokenhearted and saves those who are crushed in spirit."* Yes, I was both those things, with no place to turn but to the Lord. I had given up on myself, but He hadn't given up on me.

There's a saying in 12 Step Programs: "God does for us what we could not do for ourselves." Through the help of charities and kind-hearted Christian people, everything I'd lost was restored. God proved to me that He *does* save *"those who are crushed in spirit."*

Lord, I'm so thankful that You are true to Your word, and that You are always there when I need you. Amen.

My Thoughts and Feelings

Day Six

"But they that wait upon the Lord shall renew their strength; they shall mount up with wings as eagles; they shall run, and not be weary; and they shall walk, and not faint."

--Isa. 40:31 (KJV)

Sometimes, just because we have a mental disorder, we tend to dwell on the negative side of it instead of the positive side. And there *is* a positive side. For one thing, although bipolar disorder is a lifelong illness, at least it's not a life-threatening illness, like cancer. Another positive thing is that, if we let it, it can actually make us stronger – in character, and as people.

Hannah Whitall Smith (regarding Isa. 40:31) says: "We must use our wings, or they avail us nothing. It is not worthwhile to cry out, 'Oh that I had wings and then I would flee,' for we have the wings already, and what is needed is not more wings, but only that we should use those we have.

The power to surrender and trust exists in every human soul, and only needs to be brought into exercise. With these two wings we can 'flee' to God at any moment; but in order really to reach Him, we must actively use them."

The Scripture refers to *"mounting up with wings,"* also; however, it first refers to *"wait upon the Lord"* to *"renew [your] strength."* Many of us with bipolar disorder have realized that our own strength is not enough – many have tried to battle the disorder without medication and have failed miserably.

We must depend on God if we are to have any strength against bipolar disorder. That way we can *"mount up with wings as eagles...run, and not be weary; and...walk, and not faint."*

Not by ourselves, but as the Bible says, *"I can do everything through Him who gives me strength."* (Phil. 4:13 NIV).

Lord, help me to use my "wings" to "flee" to You whenever I need You to give me strength. Amen.

My Thoughts and Feelings

Day Seven

"These things have I spoken unto you, that my joy might remain in you, and that your joy might be full."

--John 15:11 (KJV)

The above Scripture, although recorded in the book of John, were words actually spoken by Jesus to the people – so He is talking about *His* joy here. And while in the King James Version it refers to our joy being "full," the New International Version refers to it as being "complete." As if there's nothing else we need but the joy of the Lord.

And maybe that's true – in the last reading we talked about strength; well, the Bible says, *"...for the joy of the Lord is your strength."* (Neh. 8"10b KJV/NIV).

When I've described my manic episodes to people before, I've referred to them as, "Happy-happy-joy-joy-give-me-the-checkbook-I'm-going-shopping!" But this isn't that kind of joy – it certainly is not mania.

The joy of the Lord is something that swells up from deep within you and spills out from your soul. Like, have you ever found yourself humming for no reason at all, just because you felt happy? Or singing (even along with a song)?

Would you be surprised to find out that singing as an expression of "joy unto the Lord" is nothing new – that it was done back in Bible days?

Psalms 30:4 (NIV) says, *"Sing unto the Lord, you saints of his; praise his holy name."*

Even the birds sing for joy – why shouldn't we? A.B. Simpson said, "It is the nightingale in the heart that sings at night because it is its nature to sing."

Lord, please give me Your joy, so I can sing to You, no matter what circumstances I am in. Amen.

My Thoughts and Feelings

Day Eight

"To everything there is a season, and a time to every purpose under the heaven...A time to weep and a time to laugh; a time to mourn, and a time to dance."

--Ecc. 3:1,4 (KJV)

Ok, so we can sing with joy, but can we *dance* with it? I can hear you now – "Maybe *you* can, but I can't!"

Well, everyone expresses joy in their own way (and yes, sometimes I *do* dance when I'm happy – when no one's looking, of course).

In Bible times, music was a big part of praising the Lord. Psa. 98:4-6 (KJV) says, *"Make a joyful noise unto the Lord, all the earth: make a loud noise, and rejoice, and sing praise. Sing unto the Lord with the harp; with the harp, and the voice of a psalm. With trumpets and sound of cornet make a joyful noise before the Lord, the King."*

I came upon this quote one day and I love it, because of my bipolar disorder: "Those who danced were thought quite insane by those who could not hear the music." (Angela Monet)

I told you that sometimes, when I'm real happy, I dance. Well, we have this big picture window in our living room, which happens to be where I dance. And I can just imagine what the neighbors would think if they looked in and saw me dancing! It's just like that quote says.

"Ok, I do have bipolar disorder. But I'm not as insane as I used to be!" is what I would want to yell at them.

It's like the Scripture at the top of the page says. There *is* a time to laugh. And there is also a time to dance. So dance away! (I can hear the music, and I won't think you're insane – not any more than I am, anyway!).

Lord, thank You for Your joy and the ability to express it in dance and any other way I want. Amen.

My Thoughts and Feelings

Day Nine

"...A time to weep, and a time to laugh; a time to mourn, and a time to dance."

--Ecc. 4:4 (KJV) (NIV)

There we go – one day we're weeping, and the next day we're laughing. One day we're mourning, and the next day we're dancing. Oh, those bipolar mood swings! Don't you hate them? What they used to call a "moody person," they now call "a person with bipolar disorder" (only guess which one they are more afraid of?).

Sometimes I feel like I'm so in control, and then – whap! A mood swing comes on me as fast as a hurricane. And that's a good analogy, too, because then I feel helpless, like I don't have any control over it.

I'm blessed, though. I have a husband who also has bipolar disorder, so he can see the "hurricane" coming, just like those storm trackers on TV can watch (or even predict) when a real hurricane is coming your way.

But because my husband has bipolar disorder himself, he's a wonderful supporter to me. It doesn't make the mood swings any better, but at least he's understanding about them.

Still, sometimes I question, "If I'm so spiritual, why doesn't God just take away these mood swings altogether? He knows how much I hate them."

And then I make a big mistake. I try to reason with God (like it says on TV, "Don't try this at home!"). Like I know better than He does. Like He should do what I say.

And do you know what I get in return? Nothing. Silence. Like a parent waiting for their child to be done with their tantrum.

I guess I'll just go back to quiet and willing acceptance of my bipolar disorder.

Lord, forgive me for questioning why I have bipolar disorder. I know You have a reason for everything. Amen.

My Thoughts and Feelings

Day Ten

"Verily, verily, I say unto you: That ye shall weep and lament and ye shall be sorrowful, but your sorrow shall be turned into joy."

--John 16:20 (KJV)

Anyone with bipolar disorder has had to, unfortunately, deal with the downside of the disorder – depression, sometimes a depression so deep that you can't even get out of bed. I once had a depressive episode that lasted for three weeks.

Whenever my husband would ask me what was wrong, I would answer either, "Everything," or "Nothing."

I wish I could have given a better explanation as to the reason for my depression, but I just couldn't. The fact is that I didn't know myself.

The episode came upon me with no warning, no trigger – just all of a sudden I started crying one day for seemingly no reason, and was unable to stop for three weeks.

Then, just as mysteriously as it had started, after three weeks it just stopped, and I got out of bed feeling like my "normal" self again.

I don't profess to have any understanding of this phenomenon at all – I do know that it's happened to other people with bipolar disorder, though.

The important thing is that, through it all, I never lost my faith. Even as days went into weeks, I still believed that God had a reason for letting this depression happen – if for no other reason than for me to never again take any "happy" day for granted.

I was *"sorrowful"* but, true to His word, God truly did turn my sorrow into joy when the episode passed.

Lord, thank You for showing me that even though I may experience depression from time to time, I will also experience joy. Amen.

My Thoughts and Feelings

Day Eleven

"So David and his men wept aloud until they had no strength left to weep."

--1Sam. 30:4 (NIV)

There's a difference between depression and grief. I'll never forget the day I found out the difference.

My sister Debi and I were like twins, we were so close. She was three years younger than me, so I called her the "twin of my heart." Even though we lived in separate states, Debi used to call me every morning, and we'd "have coffee together" – that's what we used to call it.

About once a month, we'd send each other "surprise packages" – boxes filled with all kinds of little things, nothing really expensive, just "sister" types of things just between us that would show the other we'd been thinking of them throughout the month.

It was a Friday. April 15th. I remember, because it was Tax Day. Debi didn't call me that morning – I "had coffee" alone. I knew she had just gotten my last "surprise box" the previous Wednesday, so I knew she wasn't mad at me or anything. Still…it was strange.

Then I got the call.

Only it wasn't my sister, it was her husband. He had come home and found her dead. She had killed herself.

I felt like someone had kicked me in the stomach – all the air went out of me.

You see, my sister Debi also had bipolar disorder, but had gone off her medications because she "felt fine" and believed she was "cured." Now she was dead.

And I felt grief. Grief, like the Scripture says, is when you weep aloud until you have no strength left to weep.

And then you weep some more.

Lord, thank You that sharing grief helps to heal that grief, and that You are with me in the midst of my grief. Amen.

My Thoughts and Feelings

Day Twelve

"David was greatly distressed...But David found strength in the Lord his God."

--1Sam. 30:6 (NIV)

Elizabeth Kubler-Ross is the leading expert on death and dying, and she came up with the five stages of grief – the first one being anger, and the last one being acceptance.

Anger? You better believe I was angry! The "twin of my heart," my sister, my best friend, was gone! She left. *She* left *me*! I felt like she left me all alone.

At that time, I had no friends, was many states away from my family, was still licking my wounds from the nasty divorce I told you about, and lived all alone – I didn't even own a pet. I thought nobody cared about me. Nobody but my sister.

And she left me all alone.

She left me, she left all of us – her husband of 21 years, her family, her friends, her clients – with no note, no explanation. She was gone. Just like that. Just like the statistic that she was.

Did you know that every year, one out of ten people with untreated bipolar disorder (people not on medication) will attempt suicide, and that one out of five will actually succeed? And these are real statistics – put out by a national organization – I didn't make them up!

So my beautiful, successful, 44-year-old, full-of-life, bipolar sister, went off her medications and became one of those one-in-five people who kill themselves.

And, like David, I was *"greatly distressed."* No, my grief went beyond that – I didn't want to live without my "twin." But, like David, I *"found strength in the Lord [my] God."*

Lord, thank You that, in my grief, You brought me the strength to bear up under it. Amen.

<u>My Thoughts and Feelings</u>

Day Thirteen

"Because thou shalt forget thy misery, and remember it as waters that pass away. Life will be brighter than noonday, and darkness will become like morning."

--Job 11:17 (NIV)

Grief is like pain – the more you share it, the more it loses its power over you. I grieved over the loss of my sister for a long time, and worked through the rest of the stages of Kubler-Ross' stages of grief.

Long before I reached the last stage of acceptance, I began sharing my sister's story.

At first it was because I felt like if I didn't, that part of me that wanted to, might just die along with her. Then I was scared of going into a bipolar episode myself.

But then I started thinking about all the lives that might be saved if people heard my sister's story and the warning for people with bipolar disorder to stay on their medications.

I talked about it, I was interviewed about it, I wrote about it on my blog, in the hopes that it might save some lives. And it has – it has saved thousands!

I did finally reach acceptance of my sister's suicide. And I know that nothing happens in God's world by mistake. Debi's death gave meaning and purpose to my life.

The more people with bipolar disorder and their supporters hear her story, the more people stay on their medications, and the more lives are saved.

I will never forget my sister but, like the Scripture says, I have forgotten my misery, *"...and remember it as waters that pass away."*

Life now *is "brighter than noonday, and darkness [has] become like morning."*

Lord, I know you give and take away. But there is always a reason. Thank You for making my sister's death count for something. Amen.

My Thoughts and Feelings

Day Fourteen

"And the peace of God, which passeth all understanding, shall keep your hearts and minds through Christ Jesus."

--Phil. 4:7 (KJV)

I used to be ashamed of having bipolar disorder. I felt like I was wearing a huge sign that everyone could see, announcing the fact that I had it.

I would imagine people pointing fingers at me and whispering to each other, "She's got bipolar disorder!" like it was some contagious disease and the CDC was going to come in and swoop me away any minute.

That's how different I felt from the rest of the world. I thought everyone else was "normal" except me.

Then I started reading in the Bible where other people were subject to emotional ups and downs themselves. Even David…and the apostles!

Peter, Paul, Isaiah, Job, and even the Lord Himself share with us in the Scriptures about their changing emotions.

I used to be ashamed of my changing emotions, until I started reading these Scriptures.

I thought that a spiritual person wouldn't feel like I did. I thought there was something wrong with my faith, something fundamentally wrong with my spirituality.

But after I read about all these great men of faith having also struggled with their changing emotions, I realized that I was in good company, and I stopped worrying about what other people thought of me.

The fact is, I do have bipolar disorder and it does come with its mood swings, but *it's NOT my fault!* I didn't do anything to cause this... I didn't do anything to deserve this.

God didn't curse me because I'm a bad Christian or because He doesn't love me. He loves me just the way I am, bipolar disorder and all. And when I realized that, I found peace with it.

Lord, thank you for loving me just the way I am, bipolar disorder and all. Amen.

My Thoughts and Feelings

Day Fifteen

"...but we glory in tribulations also; knowing that tribulation worketh patience; and patience, experience; and experience, hope."

--Rom. 5:3,4 (KJV)

Up and down.. up and down... thus go the mood swings of bipolar disorder. I made up an expression I'd really like to put on a T-shirt (if I had the nerve to wear it): "If you like rollercoasters, you'd *love* bipolar disorder!"

All kidding aside, it is very difficult to live a life so filled with *"tribulations,"* as the Scripture calls it.

We question, "Why did God pick *me* to go through such a serious, sometimes devastating, disorder? Why is it so hard for me, when I see others handling it so much easier? Why can't I seem to get a hold of this thing?"

"Why don't I ever feel like I'm in control or, even if/when I do, I lose that control so quickly? Is there something wrong with my faith? Am I not a good Christian?"

If you have asked yourself these questions (or others like them), then know that you are not alone. Many other Christians with bipolar disorder have struggled with the same things.

These are the *"tribulations"* of living with bipolar disorder, along with daily management of the disorder itself (and bipolar episodes).

But Romans 5:3,4 tells us that these tribulations have a purpose – they bring with them patience, experience, and hope. These things don't happen overnight, however.

Considering that we are impatient by nature, this is one characteristic we seem to fight. If we learn it, though, it will lead to experience.

And the more experience we have in managing our bipolar disorder, the more hope we have of long-term stability (with God's help).

Lord, it does help to know that my tribulations happen for a reason. Help me to be patient, so that experience and hope will follow. Amen.

My Thoughts and Feelings

Day Sixteen

"When you passeth through the waters, I will be with thee; and through the rivers, they shall not overflow thee. When thou walkest through the fire, thou shalt not be burned; neither shall the flame kindle upon thee."

--Isa. 43:2 (KJV)

The word that really screams out to me in this Scripture is *"overflow,"* because it speaks to me of the many, many times I have felt so *overwhelmed* by my bipolar disorder.

As Isaiah 43:2 so aptly describes it, bipolar disorder to me at times really has felt like overflowing waters or a river.

It *has* felt like I'm walking through a fire, and there have been fears of "getting burned." (I'm sure you get the analogy.)

If we dwell on our fears, worries, and negative thoughts and feelings, we *will* continue to feel as if bipolar disorder is like an overflowing river or like we're having to constantly "walk through the fire."

But God, in His mercy, does not leave us alone in our struggles – He doesn't make us deal with these overwhelming feelings all by ourselves.

Not only that, but He also promises in Isaiah 43:2 that we *will* get through it – not *maybe*, not *possibly* – He doesn't say *if*, He says *when:*

"When thou passeth through the waters..."

And He assures us that He *will* be with us. We will not be alone.

No matter how horrible these images are, there are times when we go through bipolar episodes and the feelings are just as horrible. But we are still not alone.

I know sometimes you might feel like you're all alone and overwhelmed by your bipolar disorder, but isn't it nice to know that God is right there with you?

Lord, sometimes I do feel so overwhelmed by my bipolar disorder. I'm so glad You're there to "walk through the fire" with me. Amen.

My Thoughts and Feelings

Day Seventeen

"For this God is our God for ever and ever: he will be our guide even unto death."

--Psa. 48:14 (KJV)

I was married two different times when I was 19 years old – both during manic episodes. One lasted four months and one lasted six months.

I "woke up" after each episode and it was kind of like, "Who are you, and what is this ring doing on my finger?"

That was back when I didn't even know what bipolar disorder was, much less that I had it. But now that I look back, I know I did, and I know that's what it was. It's a matter of, "I wish I knew then what I know now."

When we're at that age, we don't always make the best decisions anyway – many of them are impulsive ones.

Couple that with a bipolar manic episode, where you're also dealing with the possibility of rash and poor decision-making capabilities, distorted thinking, impulsive and risk-taking behavior, and the other symptoms of a manic episode – and you have a recipe for disaster!

I've had multiple marriages because of my bipolar disorder, and they were mistakes. Well, actually, the biggest mistake of all was relying on my own judgment (faulty at best).

Psalms 48:14 tells us that God *"will be our guide even unto death."*

Maybe if I had sought *God's* guidance, instead of my own faulty, impulsive, poor decision-making, I wouldn't have made the bad choices that I made.

Lord, help me to do better at seeking Your guidance first, before I make mistakes that I regret later. Amen.

My Thoughts and Feelings

Day Eighteen

"Be not wise in thine own eyes: fear the Lord, and depart from evil."

--Prov. 3:7 (KJV)

Mistakes. We all make them. The important thing is what we do about them.

Do we let them make us bitter or better? Do we dwell on our mistakes, beating ourselves over the head with them, or do we learn from them? Do we keep repeating the same mistakes over and over again, or do we change ourselves so that we don't?

There's a saying that goes, "If nothing changes, nothing changes." If you don't see "the error of your ways," you'll never change.

And that's not bipolar disorder, that's insanity, because the common definition of insanity is "doing the same thing over and over again, expecting different results."

You can't change the fact that you have bipolar disorder. You may not even have control over some of the mistakes that you make during a bipolar episode. But what you do have control over is your ability to change.

You may not be able to change your circumstances, but you *can* change your *reaction* to them.

Change is another word for "transformed."

So, maybe, by changing yourself, your circumstances *can* be transformed into something you can live with or learn from.

Psalms 3:7 says to *"...fear the Lord and depart from evil."*

In other words, depend on God and stop making the same mistakes over and over again.

Lord, I don't want to keep making the same mistakes over and over again. I know I can change with Your help. Amen.

My Thoughts and Feelings

Day Nineteen

It's not uncommon for people with bipolar disorder to forget what they've said or done during a bipolar episode. But boy are they surprised sometimes when the episode is over and they're looking at devastation as severe as the after-effects of a great hurricane!

Sometimes spouses are not as forgiving as God is, especially if the episode involved infidelity. Or friends, if you've embarrassed them in public.

Or your children, if you've acted inappropriately in front of their friends, especially at school.

What about the credit card companies? You may have forgotten that shopping spree you went on during your manic episode, but they didn't. Neither did the bank, when you overdrew your checking account.

The hard part is that, even though you may have forgotten what you said or did during the episode, blaming your behavior on bipolar disorder is no excuse.

You still have to take responsibility and apologize to those people you hurt, and repay debts you incurred.

I was once in a bipolar episode so bad that I had to have ECT (Electro-Convulsive Therapy) – shock treatments – because my medications had stopped working for me.

I forgot an entire Thanksgiving! To this day, I can't remember a thing that happened that day.

But with all that said, isn't it a comfort to know that, no matter what, God will *never* forget us? Isaiah 49:15,16 assures us of that.

Lord, though my memory may be faulty and I might forget things, I am so grateful that You will never forget me. Amen.

My Thoughts and Feelings

Day Twenty

"For the Lord comforts his people and will have compassion on his afflicted ones."

--Isa. 49:13 (NIV)

Sometimes, having bipolar disorder really gets to me. I mean, it's not like I had a choice – if I did, I would have picked a more "popular" illness, one more glamorous, one that at least had a yearly telethon for it! Or at least one that had a cure for it.

No, I definitely would not have chosen to have bipolar disorder.

People still consider it such a bad mental illness; it still has such a negative connotation to it. And people are still so afraid of those of us who have it, just like they were of the lepers back in Bible times.

Sometimes I feel like I have control over my "mental illness," but other times I truly feel "mentally ill." I feel "different." I feel "abnormal." I feel isolated – a societal outcast.

Like the Scripture says, sometimes I feel like an *"afflicted one."*

But the Scripture also says that God will have compassion on his afflicted ones.

Did you hear that? God will have compassion on us. On *us*! Those people who have bipolar disorder, a mental illness, who society shuns – the "afflicted ones" – *those* are the people upon whom God will have compassion.

It also says that He will *comfort* us.

Now that makes me feel better.

God Himself will comfort me. I don't need anyone else to comfort me.

Lord, when I feel "afflicted" because of my bipolar disorder, it's so nice to know that You will comfort me. Amen.

My Thoughts and Feelings

Day Twenty-One

"Trust in the Lord with all thine heart, and lean not on thine own understanding. In all thy ways acknowledge him, and he shall direct thy paths."

--Prov. 3:5,6 (KJV)

I never trusted anyone. Not from the time I was 12 years old, anyway, and was molested by an acquaintance of my father's.

I didn't want to tell anyone, thinking that somehow it was my fault.

I've long since made peace with what happened that day, but I still think it was the event that triggered my life of self-destruction and abusive relationships.

Because I never trusted anyone, I think that's one of the reasons it took so long for me to finally get a correct diagnosis of bipolar disorder.

I saw many psychiatrists, counselors, and therapists over the years, but because I didn't trust any of them, I just told them what I thought they wanted to hear. I was so afraid someone would find out my secret.

I received diagnoses from my first one of major depression at 16 years old, to schizophrenia, to MPD (Multiple Personality Disorder), to PTSD (Post-Traumatic Stress Disorder), to ADHD (Attention Deficit Hyperactivity Disorder), to OCD (Obsessive Compulsive Disorder), to

BPD (Borderline Personality Disorder)… if it had letters in it, I was diagnosed with it!

Finally at 44 years old, I was diagnosed with bipolar disorder and put on the right medications and on my way to stability.

Because I finally trusted someone.

Like Proverbs 3:5 says, I trusted in the Lord. People had always let me down, I'd thought, but God had never let me down.

I was tired of the lie I was living. I was tired of *"leaning on my own understanding."* So I trusted God.

He directed my path then, and He still directs my path today – the path of stability and serenity.

Lord, I'm so glad that I can trust You. I'm grateful that You never let me down. Amen.

My Thoughts and Feelings

Day Twenty-Two

"...Fear not: for I have redeemed thee, I have called thee by name; thou art mine."

--Isa. 43:1 (KJV)

"Hi, my name is Michele, and I have bipolar disorder."

Thus was my introduction to my bipolar support group (I felt like I was in a 12-Step Program). I was hesitant to even give my name, even though no one knew me there. And I did not want to say that I had bipolar disorder, because that meant I could no longer be in denial of it.

Even as each person went around and did the same thing, I felt like I was expected to feel as if I now belonged.

But the truth was, I didn't *want* to belong. I didn't even want to be there! I not only had a bad disorder, I had a bad attitude! I was angry – I did *not* want to be like "them."

Until someone told *my* story.

As they shared what living with bipolar disorder had been like for them, I could relate.

Then another person shared... and another. And I realized I was more like "them" than I knew.

It was like coming home. Finally, I'd found a group of people who understood me.

When they called me by my name, they weren't calling me by my patient number or my disorder. They were recognizing me for who I am.

I finally *belonged* somewhere! I wasn't alone and afraid any more.

That's how I feel when I read Isaiah 43:1. God says, *"Fear not."* I'm not afraid any more.

He says, *"I have called thee by name; thou art mine."* He calls me by my name, and I not only belong, I belong to *Him*!

Lord, thank You that I'm not alone and afraid any more. I'm so grateful that I belong to You. Amen.

My Thoughts and Feelings

Day Twenty-Three

*"When anxiety was great within me, your consolation
brought joy to my soul."*

--Psa. 94:19 (NIV)

So many people with bipolar disorder are also diagnosed
with some type of anxiety disorder; or, if not formally
diagnosed, at least still have to deal with anxiety.

I used to have full-blown anxiety attacks before anti-
anxiety medication became part of my "sanity cocktail"
(that's what I call my medications).

Many people who don't understand bipolar disorder don't
think anxiety is such a big deal – they don't understand the
absolutely paralyzing control it can have over you – the
panic that can keep you from doing even the most "normal"
of things that people without bipolar disorder can do.

After I had my "meltdown" at the hospital where I worked
as a medical transcriptionist, it was *years* before I could
even get near that street without having an anxiety attack!

Even as far back as grammar school, I remember feeling
anxiety.

I didn't know what it was called, of course. Some people
call it "butterflies in your stomach" (what an innocuous
term). I called it, "that feeling that something is going to
go wrong today" – much les innocuous; more like fear
personified, and at such a young age.

It wasn't until much later in life, after I was diagnosed with bipolar disorder, that I found the Scripture of Psalms 94:19.

I knew what it was like *"when anxiety was great within me,"* but then I found the consolation of the Lord, which *did* bring joy to my soul.

Lord, thank You that when I do feel anxious, You are there to console me and to bring me joy. Amen.

My Thoughts and Feelings

Day Twenty-Four

"Casting all your care upon him, for he careth for you."

--1Pet. 5:7 (KJV)

"Cast all your anxiety upon him because he cares for you."

--1Pet. 5:7 (NIV)

Webster's dictionary calls anxiety a "fearful concern."

I had so many "fearful concerns" that it was no wonder I spent so much of my time depressed. If you worried about all the things I worried about, you'd be depressed, too!

The problem is not that we care, but that we care too much. And about the wrong things. We worry about the past – over which we can do nothing about (except learn from and go on), and we fear the future – over which we can do nothing about, because it isn't here yet.

These are things that cause us anxiety. These are things that cause us fear. These are things that cause us depression.

Sometimes anxiety and fear can so overpower those of us with bipolar disorder that we "take to our beds," overcome with the cares of the world (our world). And that's when it becomes dangerous – because then we can isolate.

And isolation is one of the biggest triggers to a bipolar episode. What's worse is that, in isolating, we may have cut ourselves off from the very people who could have helped us.

But no matter how isolated or depressed we become, the one person we are never cut off from is God.

He tells you to cast all your care/anxiety ("fearful concern") on Him, *"because he cares for you."*

No matter what is going on, no matter how overwhelmed or scared you are, remember that God cares for *you!*

Lord, I am so glad that I can cast all my care and anxiety on You, because sometimes it's just too much for me to handle alone. Amen.

My Thoughts and Feelings

Day Twenty-Five

"Do not be anxious about anything, but in everything, by prayer and petition, with thanksgiving, present your requests to God. And the peace of God, which transcends all understanding, will guard your hearts and your minds in Christ Jesus."

--Phil. 4:6,7 (NIV)

I'm what they call an ultra-rapid cycler. That means with my type of bipolar disorder, I can go from manic to depressed in 60 seconds flat! No, I'm only kidding – it doesn't happen that fast.

But seriously, it does mean that, unlike mixed bipolar episodes, where you can experience symptoms of both mania and depression at the same time – I can go from mania to depression to mania and back again in the *same day*! It can be both frustrating and confusing.

And very emotionally draining. Imagine how you feel after one bipolar episode – after one set of mood swings. Now imagine how you'd feel after a whole day of constant mood swings!

One minute you're laughing, the next minute you're crying. And the worst part is that you have no control over it.

I also have the kind of bipolar disorder that comes with psychotic features. So, yes, I would hear voices in my mind.

At first I would joke about it – I got a keychain that said, "I do what the voices inside my head tell me to," and a T-shirt that said, "I hear voices, and they don't like you."

But then it wasn't funny any more. I just wanted the voices to stop. I just wanted *peace*.

Philippians 4:6,7 says that I can pray and present my requests to God. I did.

But I also went into the hospital, where they gave me medication.

Medication doesn't give you peace, however – only God can – the peace *"which transcends all understanding,"* and *"...will guard...your mind."*

The voices stopped. And I still have the peace of God.

Lord, thank You for doctors who could heal my mind, but thank You for Your spiritual healing which gives peace to my heart. Amen.

My Thoughts and Feelings

Day Twenty-Six

*"Have mercy on me, O God, have mercy on me, for in you
my soul takes refuge. I will take refuge in the shadow of
your wings until the disaster has passed."*

--Psa. 57:1 (NIV)

My last hospitalization was because of a manic episode that
medication at home was unable to bring me out of, and I
was scared.

What was worse was that I was scaring my husband, and I
would never do anything to hurt him. So I agreed to go
into the hospital until the episode was over.

Because I was in such a controlled (safe) environment, they
found the right medications for me quickly, I got the
therapy I needed, and I was able to go home after less than
a week, episode-free.

The point is, though, that a manic episode *should* scare you.
It certainly scares your family and your supporter. You
may like the "high feeling" of the mania, but your supporter
is afraid for you, afraid of what it does to you, afraid of
what you might do because of it.

My husband wasn't afraid *of* me because, after all, I'm all of
4'10" and he's 6'5", but he sure was afraid *for* me.

Every day he watched me get worse and worse. As you
will, too, if you go into a manic episode and don't get help
for it.

Even if you don't think of yourself, think of your family and what it does to them. Then get the help you need.

Psalms 57:1 says, *"I will take refuge in the shadow of your wings until the disaster has passed."* The disaster, in my case, was my manic episode.

Yes, I went into the hospital – it was the right thing to do for my body. But I took refuge in the shadow of the wings of God – it was the right thing to do for my soul.

Lord, when my bipolar disorder is out of control, I am so grateful that I can take refuge in You until the disaster has passed. Amen.

My Thoughts and Feelings

Day Twenty-Seven

"I cry out to God Most High, to God, who fulfills his purpose for me."

--Psa. 57:2 (NIV)

"Why does this bipolar disorder have to interfere with my life so much?" I wanted to scream. "Why can't I just be normal? Why can't I just be ME?"

I thought that having bipolar disorder had ruined my whole life - my future - any hopes I had for a "normal" life.

I hated the thought of having to take medication for the rest of my life. I thought of *myself* as broken, instead of my *brain* as broken.

No future. That's what I thought – no future. So I gave up on the present.

I lost all motivation, any desire to make anything of myself or my life. I gave up on my dreams. And I blamed it on the bipolar disorder.

I had no purpose. Proverbs 29:18 (KJV) says, *"Where there is no vision, the people perish..."* Oh, I was perishing, all right.

No more visions, dreams, hopes, wishes... I was now "damaged goods."

How was I going to become the writer I'd always hoped to be, when I never knew if/when the hallucinations (voices) would come back and I'd write gibberish?

How could I trust that the Coffeehouse I'd hoped to someday open wasn't just a "grandiose idea" thought up during a manic episode?

I cried. I cried out. And I finally cried out to God, "Dear Lord, what is Your purpose for me?"

And in spite of my bipolar disorder and my own self-doubts, God was still true to His word of Psalms 57:2, and today I am the writer I always dreamed of being.

Lord, thank You that even though I lost my way for awhile, You still fulfilled Your purpose for me. Amen.

My Thoughts and Feelings

Day Twenty-Eight

*"For I know the plans I have for you, declares the Lord,
plans to prosper you and not to harm you, plans to give you
hope and a future."*

--Jer. 29:11 (NIV)

When you were little, what did you want to be when you grew up – a fireman or policeman? An astronaut? A ballerina? The president?

Of course, I'm probably showing my age here. Nowadays, children want to grow up to be famous actors or actresses, wrestlers, or CEO's of Fortune 500 companies. But the point is that they have dreams. And we had dreams as children.

Don't let bipolar disorder steal your dreams. Of course, you probably don't still dream of being that ballerina or being the president. But you can have realistic dreams. Dreams with a hope and a future.

Even if your previous dreams have been waylaid because you had to go on disability because of your bipolar disorder, you can still have new dreams – even better dreams! But they have to be realistic dreams. And they may take some help to make them come true.

Dreams first start with a thought (or maybe a wish). But then they take planning. Goals – long- term goals that you meet by a series of short-term goals. And, like I said, the help of others.

The biggest help you'll get is from the Lord. Seek *His* guidance first, because He knows His plans for you – He says so in Jeremiah 29:11.

He also says that those plans include *prospering* you, not harming you, and plans *"to give you hope and a future."*

Don't let bipolar disorder steal your dreams. Let God give you new ones.

Lord, please show me the plans You have for me. Give me new dreams, so I can have hope and a future. Amen.

My Thoughts and Feelings

Day Twenty-Nine

*"For God hath not given us the spirit of fear, but of power,
and of love, and of a sound mind."*

--2Tim.1:7 (KJV)

There were times when I literally thought I'd lost my mind (and was afraid I wouldn't get it back).

Have you ever been so far into a bipolar episode that you were afraid you'd never come back? Kind of like Dorothy in Oz, isn't it? We just want to "come home."

It took two years for them to get me stable on my medications (my "sanity cocktail"). But it was mostly my fault.

I would be medication compliant for awhile, but then I'd go off my medications because I missed my manic "highs" so much.

Then, of course, I would go into a manic episode and we'd have to start all over again. Can you see the insanity in that (I couldn't)?

Again, like I said in the "mistakes" reading, the definition of insanity being "doing the same thing over and over again expecting different results."

I guess I was afraid, like many people when they're first diagnosed with bipolar disorder, that the medications would take away my personality- somehow "deaden" that part that made me, well, *me.*

Like I wouldn't be myself any more – I'd just be some kind of bipolar disorder wind-up robot, doing what the doctors told me to do. When, in fact, the opposite is true. On the right medications, in the right dosages, I'm a better "me" than I ever was before!

2Timothy 1:7 says that God hasn't given me a spirit of fear – so I don't have to be afraid of the hospital, doctors, medications, or even being me.

It also says that God has given me a sound mind. See? A *sound mind!* I haven't lost my mind after all!

Lord, thank You for giving me a sound mind so that any time I'm afraid I'm losing it, I can remember that I really do have a sound mind. Amen.

My Thoughts and Feelings

Day Thirty

"Be content with what you have, because God has said,
'Never will I leave you; never will I forsake you."

--Heb. 13:5 (NIV)

"...and, lo, I am with you always, even unto the end of the
world. Amen."

--Matt. 28:20 (KJV)

If I were to leave you with one last thought, it would be this: YOU ARE NOT ALONE!

The fact that over 10 million people in this country are touched by bipolar disorder may not mean much to you. The fact that there are others with bipolar disorder may not mean much to you. The fact that you have bipolar disorder means everything to you.

Still, you may feel alone.

For most of my life I was alone and lonely. I would feel alone in a room full of people. Because I always felt different...strange...dysfunctional...broken...damaged goods. It wasn't until I found the Lord that I no longer felt alone.

Bipolar support groups were fine – for the "outside" me. But I still had an ache in my heart – a spiritual loneliness that nothing could fill. My bipolar disorder drove everyone away, and I was alone anyway. But there was one person who *never* left me – God. He says in Hebrews 13:5, *"Never will I leave you; never will I forsake you,"* and He has proven that to me.

Living with bipolar disorder is not easy, but DON'T GIVE UP!

You do NOT have to face this alone, whether you have a supporter or not. Matthew 28:20 tells you that.

In it, God Himself says to you, *"...and, lo, I am with you always, even unto the end of the world. Amen."* And Amen.

I wish you happiness, and I wish you stability.

Lord, thank You that I am not alone and never will be again. Thank You that You will always be with me. Amen.

My Thoughts and Feelings

The Rest of Your Life

"He who dwells in the shelter of the Most High will rest in the shadow of the Almighty. I will say of the Lord, 'He is my refuge and my fortress, my God, in whom I trust'...He will cover you with his feathers, and under his wings you will find refuge: his faithfulness will be your shield and rampart."

--Psa. 91:1,2,4 (NIV)

My dear friend,

I hope this book has been an inspiration to you and given you hope that you can carry with you for the rest of your life.

Everyone has a story to tell, and each day we write a few more lines of it. What will the end of your story be? If you trust in the Lord, no doubt it will have a happy ending, because He is faithful and *"under his wings you will find refuge..."*

"He is my refuge and my fortress, my God, in whom I trust..."

Even if you have never trusted anyone else before, you *can* trust in God. He is your Heavenly Father, who loves you with the love a parent has for their child. He wants only the best for you.

Will your future be without struggle? Unfortunately, no. We all struggle. Will you survive? Yes. Will you be better for it? I hope so. I believe in the saying, "That which doesn't kill you makes you stronger."

There is something so soothing about the words, *"He will cover you with his feathers, and under his wings you will find refuge..."* So many of us who struggle with bipolar disorder have had experiences where we didn't feel safe at all. Isn't it nice to know that, in God, you can be safe?

If you have yet to make God your Lord and Savior, I encourage you to do it now. Put your life into His hands, and trust the promises He has made to you. He will *not* let you down.

May the rest of your life be one filled with happiness and stability, as you grow in your spiritual walk and recover from your bipolar disorder.

Yours in Christ,

Michele

Michele Sexton has a blog for survivors of bipolar disorder at: www.bipolarsurvivor-michele.blogspot.com

For more information on Michele, her other books, or personal appearances and speaking engagements, please contact her at: brokenroseministries@gmail.com

or visit the website at: www.brokenroseministries.com

Made in the USA
Monee, IL
16 November 2020